messages
undelivered
tiffany gregory

messages
undelivered

Tiffany Gregory is thrilled to share *Messages Undelivered,* her first poetry collection. This is an exploration of love, loss, healing, and unspoken words carried. Letters she thought she would never deliver, buried confessions uncovered, and whispers of vulnerability she had only revealed to herself. Tiffany believes that even the messiest moments contain powerful messages that carry meaning. Through this work, she hopes you find healing in the pain, the strength to believe in love again, and most importantly, the courage to choose yourself. Her wish is that this collection helps turn pain into closure, using hurt as a starting point for healing and transformation. Tiffany hopes you recognize the good that surrounds you and know the future you dream of creating is achievable. Never silence the voices of your heart, but rather share these messages with the world.

to the ones who
hurt me,
lost me,
see me,
love me

introduction

"For some reason, I'm having a hard time getting over things and people who have hurt me. I've noticed I've used these situations to fuel my dreams, but I no longer want to use pain as motivation. How do I let this go?"

I shared these words during a remote session with my therapist. We began to workshop ideas, and the one that stuck with me was simple: *write letters.*

After my session ended, I pulled out three pieces of paper and wrote letters to three people who had hurt me immensely, and in different but significant ways. I wrote angrily, sadly, and intentionally. These letters were addressed directly to them. I couldn't write fast enough. It felt like I was going to explode. As I sat at my desk, tears fell onto the pages, but I didn't stop my hand. I couldn't. I didn't want to stop. I was finally saying everything I needed and wanted to say but never had the opportunity to. This was it! Once I felt somewhat satisfied, I read the messages aloud and then added more.

Writing the letters was planned. What happened next was not. Something whispered to me: *"Now, burn them."* I reached for a lighter, sat on my empty apartment patio, and lit the words on fire. Watching them burn to ash filled me with an unexpected sense of satisfaction. Once it was finished, I felt a release. I needed it, and I wanted to keep feeling that energy.

Though I literally couldn't tell you what the original three letters said, I decided to keep writing messages to the people and situations that had hurt me no matter how many times I had to revisit them, because getting over things isn't linear.

For months, I wrote every single day until one day, I felt like the burning sadness was no longer great enough to consume me. Still, I discovered there were more messages I wanted to write.

I thought if I could write all these grievances to people who tried to break me, I could surely write to the ones who helped rebuild me, believed in me, loved me, saw my ugly, and still decided to stay. These are my friends and family who saved me, even when I felt I was beyond worthy of any type of redemption. I wanted to write to God. Though I still haven't written enough, and these words could never express the rawness and realness I feel for these souls, I tried. I also felt I should write to the ones I've hurt, bruised, pained, and abandoned. I'm not perfect, nor do I pretend to be.

Lastly, I realized I needed to write to the person I've treated the worst, the most poorly, most unfairly, and at times, with deliberate cruelty. I needed to write to me. Negative self-talk is something I regrettably inherited, and I'm choosing to stop. I'm choosing to stop shaming myself for simply being human. I'm choosing to stop editing myself to be liked and accepted. I will no longer mute myself to satisfy voices that do not belong to me. I'll no longer be my own judge and jury of shame.

Though they are not addressed to individuals by name, this is me finally sending the letters. This is a release and a reminder that even unsent words can set us free. This is my release and hopefully, it becomes a part of yours.

contents

messages
unsent

there's so much i've been wishing to tell you
but was too afraid to press send
things have been over between us for a while now
but it feels like the grieving won't end

there's so much i've been wishing to tell you
but was too afraid to press send
i'm exhausted from repeatedly getting over you
time and time again

there's so much i've been wishing to tell you
but was too afraid to press send
my heart was a closed door
but somehow you got in

there's so much i've been wishing to tell you
but was too afraid to press send
if i'd known we'd eventually be nothing to each other
i would have never let things begin

i'm not a hoodie.

you can't just try me on and put me back after you're done, if i don't fit.

i'm not a piece of clothing.

i'm not like that old button-down in the back of your closet that you are saving in case the rotation of t-shirts just isn't doing it for you. i refuse to be a part of your wardrobe.

the article you put on when you want to feel comfortable. the one that's worn out and torn because you didn't know how to handle me with care. the one you are too afraid to simply let go of because, one day, you might need me. the one you desperately search for when you need dependability.

i know i'm full of memories and have overlooked all the stains accumulated over the years, but i deserve to be repaired, stitched, washed, and released. i have no doubt someone *will value me* as treasure and not trash. for some reason, you're too scared to let me go or to simply wear me. to let me influence your style. allow my presence to complement and highlight your best features.

it's clear that you don't want me. still, you hold on to me by a thread. and sometimes, it feels like when you finally release me...i'll unravel.

i'm starting to see a pattern
a template on which i trace the best parts of you
to fit onto me
unfortunately, that's not how love works
you can't just draw what you like
and erase the rest as if it doesn't exist
people aren't written in pencil
people are bled with pen

i'm starting to see a familiar thread
stitched through every love line
the seams start off consistent
and somehow become crooked

as i try to correct the sketch
there are always marks
from the unsuccessful do-overs
no matter how careful the attempt
the clean lines never stay straight

i repeatedly fall in love
with versions of you i've unknowingly drafted
i'll just dull the edges here
i'll lighten the shadows there
only to find my revisions
can never measure up
to the scribbles of your imperfections

you left a mark on me that can't be erased
not the kind that fades over time
the kind that becomes one with my skin
tattooed on my soul
in a place no one else can touch
~ *written in ink*

at one point i was unsure i was able to
experience anything
i was numb
untouched by joy
unmoved by pain
existing but not living
drifting in nothingness
but then you appeared
you stirred up emotions
i thought no longer belonged to me
you made me *feel*

after our first conversation
i believed one day you'd be mine
if not right now at some point
our paths would align
this connection somehow felt divine
like we were created for each other
under cosmic design

there's just something magnetic between us
an energy that attracts us to each other regardless of
space, distance, or time
it's like i've known you all along
it's strange how a person can come around and you forget
what your life was like before they did
~ *kinetic connection*

sometimes love blooms in unexpected places
through trauma, grief, and in-between phases
the spaces we try to leave untouched
in the recollection that *still* hurts so much

it meets us where we are
not where we pretend to be
accepts the version of us
we don't want others to see

it shows up with scars hidden by thorns
if we let the guards down
true connection can form

friendship that ignites into love is rare
you and i make an indubitable pair
conversing for hours with unlimited things to share
getting lost in creativity without any care

you see the world through a lens mirroring mine
two parallel souls, somehow aligned
when we are together, our spirits combine
our minds operate harmoniously
tangled and intertwined
~ *twin flame*

when i'm with you, i forget other people exist
it's like we are the only ones in the room
your eyes swallow me in their abyss
i've never wanted more to be consumed

something about being in your arms
literally made me dissolve
in your embrace there was no problem
that couldn't be solved
you took away all my doubt
at least when i was in your presence
but when we were apart
that feeling was
evanescent

"i feel you when i'm with you."
make me melt why don't you

somehow your words have touched me more
than your hands have

i don't know when
but sometime between the conversation
the laughing
the kissing
and the cuddling
i fell unexpectedly

it wasn't this earthquake
or a catastrophic moment
but a quiet awakening

a peaceful breeze that whispered in my ears
softly brushing over my heart

it was like time slowed
and in that stillness
i finally noticed

you

i've ruminated about kissing you
way more than i'd like to admit
about your lips
nearly impossible to forget
the way they feel
how they taste
the way they look
their perfect shape
even in my own mind
i'm unable to escape
this fantasy of you
somehow i've made

the ocean's depth can never compare
to the way you kissed me so deeply
how you held my face
as i looked into the constellations of your eyes so sweetly
for you i was falling so far
that i couldn't tell if i was among seashells or stars
your love pulls me like the moon draws the sea
dancing in the tides where there's no gravity
drifting in an ocean of galaxies
there's nowhere else
no other places
i'd rather be

sometimes when i'm with other people
i think about you
but when i'm with you
other people don't exist

seems like we feel the same heat
burning at the same time
crackling in the space between us
but neither of us dare acknowledge the electricity
we speak in connected glances
in sensual touches
every inhale a question
every exhale a statement

until

the tension grows heavy with desire
the air grows thick with want
making our breaths shallow
and the loud silence unbearable
a fire built up
now ready to explode

you rejected me before things even began
you said it was about timing but now i understand
i see it for what it is, though you tried to camouflage
you destroyed something so good...this is

sabotage

you pulled me in only to step away
you let me go when i hoped that you'd stay
you made me believe you weren't the same
you left me feeling such familiar pain
as all the others did in my past
when in fact you did what they did... exact
i should have known this wouldn't last
because i came in bare-faced while you wore a mask

don't say you cared when you never let us grow
don't say you liked me when you so easily let me go

before we even had a chance to breathe
you ended things as soon as i expressed my needs
stepped in front and asked to be seen
it seems like you wanted things to come with ease
but easy just isn't
me

in the end, you said you weren't ready to commit, but what you really meant was you weren't ready to commit to me. i'm still trying to make it all make sense.

there was a time when people said, *"i'm not looking for anything serious."* it was clean. honest. they'd lay it on the table, casually, no sugar. i could respect that even if i couldn't accept it.

but you...

you met up with me, just not on dates. you'd talked to me for hours, yet it was never long enough for me to feel known. you kept me at arm's length, surface level, because going any deeper might drown you.

you wouldn't share your trauma, but you wanted mine
you wouldn't let me in, but you wanted to be inside me
you blurred lines between situationship and relationship
you let me fall for you with no intentions to catch me

nowadays it's different; it's worse
it's no longer enough for someone to lust after my body
they want to taste my soul
they want to take up space in my heart
learn every corner of me
just to throw it away

as if it meant nothing
as if we were nothing
as if i were nothing

i fell in love with the idea of you
not who you truly are
love built on illusion
a story my mind crafted in delusion
~ *limerence*

i romanticized you so badly
i saw everything except what was exactly in front of me
you'd say something and i'd try to justify it
you were inconsistent and i stayed silent

you were a beautiful fantasy i designed in my brain
so when you couldn't live up to it
i had no one to blame

i had on rose-colored goggles with delulu frames
i tried to make things work, but it takes two to change
a situationship... i mean, situation
but i want a relationship and you just want relations

33

you make me forget
everything i said i wouldn't do
all those *"girl i could never"*
i'd do them for you
and i did
why were you the exception to my rules?
i let every boundary down
and that's how things got out of hand
because if i don't protect me
then who can?

i don't want to color outside the lines
when it comes to love
either we are in or out no in between
you think it's black and white
but the colors i dream
could paint a beautiful picture

i'm not saying things have to be perfect
to be great,
or that i won't say something stupid
make a bad choice or a mistake

i want to be real with you
and define the lines
so that in no way in your head
or in mine
we have to ask *"what are we?"*

i want us to see each other's blues when we are down
greens when we are jealous
reds when we are lustful
yellows when we are joyful
and every other color that puts the art in our hearts

i want my hues and saturation to bleed bright in your eyes
my vibrancy and highlights to make you feel alive
inspire you to live boldly and big
start painting again

when i see you
i love the view
and every shape, color, and shade of you
so why can't our relationship be defined in this way

35

how can you trace my body
with your fingers and still not be drawn to me?
can't you picture the art
we could make

i'm starting to realize
you only want me on your terms

it was a hard lesson to accept
but i learned
that you like to come and go as you please
pick me up
and put me down with ease
string me along just enough
that it feels like you are meeting my needs
when clearly you are not
and don't have the capacity
to straight up just stop

it's partly on me because if you were any other guy
you'd be blocked and no longer have access
but for some reason i keep the door open for you
and it's hard to accept
that i'm still waiting
for you to come in

i searched my body
for traces of you
for your fingerprints
the residue of your kisses
the perfume of your scent
i want to erase every place
your hands and your lips have been
and to forget
they'll never touch me
again

i never believed in *right person wrong time*
until i met you

but there's no such thing as right person wrong time
all time is now
if it's not the right time

you're the wrong person

you told me i wasn't what you were looking for romantically, but then later you come back to me like something had changed.

now i know that was a lie. and even though i should have believed you the first time, i wanted to give us a real try.

you *acted right* for a brief period of time. you showed up. you acted like you cared. just long enough for me to become hopeful then went back to old patterns.

what did i do to make you think that i'm just an option?

i deserve effort.
i deserve presence.
i deserve care.
so no.
bare minimum, low effort, carelessness doesn't count.

you were never mine
but i grieved you
like you belonged to me.
how can someone who never possessed my heart
shatter it?

i miss calling you
i miss hearing your voice
i miss telling our dreams
i miss sharing our joys
i miss giving our time
i miss showing our flaws
i miss seeing you smile
i miss you
i miss it all.

you were emotionally unavailable every time i called
~ *flat line*

i believe that in some universe, we end up together.
~ *you belong with me*

i know you want to be friends
but seeing you become someone who doesn't want me
romantically is unbearable

i do wish we could be friends
but i won't pretend that you meant nothing to me

there are so many reasons
i can't just be friends with you

i can't pretend that you mean nothing to me
can't look at you without seeing a future that could be
can't listen to you laugh without getting butterflies
can't look in your eyes and not be mesmerized
can't watch you speak without wanting to kiss
can't hear your voice without making a wish
can't be near you without wanting to touch
can't embrace you without thinking of us

i can't be friends with you
because i want so much more
not just some of you
but all of you

45

even though i hadn't seen you in a while
it felt like no time had passed at all

my body remembered

you

the way your kisses melt into my skin
how your eyes search familiar places
your hands just know where to lie
our breaths synced like a song
hearts beating to the same rhythm

it's as if i knew you'd return,
and was waiting
my body knows you by heart

you take up so much space in my mind
you can't live rent free here

be honest
do you ever think about me?

i wonder, do we ever think about each other
at the same time

you must be thinking about me
because you are the only thing in my brain
some nights i lie in bed and memories just rewind
until i fall asleep
and even in my dreams they play on repeat
please stop trying to meet me in my thoughts
i'm trying to forget you and all that was lost

47

as much as i try to act like i'm over you

i'm not.

and i can't help but wonder
did you feel anything for me at all?

was it all an act
was any of it real
even for a moment
or were you using me to fill the emptiness
until something
until someone
better came along

i grieve the memories we didn't make
the time we haven't spent
the life we never lived
and the love we will never know
~ *never together*

i can hear it
people growing tired of me
because your name is the only word i speak
the only word i seem to remember

my friends tell me i deserve better
and someone amazing will come along
when i least expect it

but they never witnessed the way i melted in your arms
they didn't feel this fever you left burning in my chest
they never had the experience of looking in your
big beautiful eyes
as you lied
to me

relationships are about two people choosing each other
but somehow i chose you
and you chose someone else

it hurts so deeply
that i can't even cry
with every inhale my chest aches
with pressure that i just
can't seem to exhale

a month ago
i was laying in your bed
and today
you're lying in someone else's arms
at first i was devastated
but now i'm grateful
seeing you with someone else made me realize
you would have destroyed me

i'm so tired of repeatedly getting over you.

i'll never share all my favorite places with someone again
because every time i visit them i remember you aren't here
and i'm trying to forget that *you ever were*

how did we go from strangers
to you living in every corner
of my mind

every choice i make
somehow circles back to you,
and it's crazy because
we haven't even discussed
what this is
i'd like to think you are mine

but people don't belong to us
we do not own each other
we are just two souls
crossing paths for however long

it's a blessing that we are
allowed to experience one
another even if only for a
short piece
of time

55

there's a softness i have for you
no matter how hard my heart hurts

maybe we were never meant to be, but how can that be true? i just don't believe it: not from the way we laugh, the way we kiss, the way we talk for hours. if i had one wish, i'd pray you'd be mine, no matter how long it took, even for a short time. i'd love the chance to show you the truest romance. even as "just friends," i'm in such a trance when i'm in your presence. how can you not see what's clearly visible? i guess because i haven't said it aloud.

i'm in love with you.

i said, *"your guilt consumes you, yet i feel nothing at all."*

what i meant to say was, *"the pain i feel hurts so deeply that it began to drown me."* to keep breathing, my brain taught my heart to become still, almost beatless. i didn't stop feeling by choice. i did it to survive losing you. i did it to protect myself, and to do that, i had to make myself numb. i had to make myself feel nothing.

i showed you all of me, and still, it wasn't enough
i had nothing left to give
i gave it all to you
i thought i could trust you with my darkest secrets
i stripped my sadness before your eyes
i let you touch the depths of my soul
i allowed you to kiss the trauma scars
and somehow, after you saw me completely unclothed
you decided i looked better dressed
~ *shamefully naked*

no one has hurt me more than you and no one ever will again

i know i made it look easy but leaving you hurt me more
than you can imagine
~ *i chose me*

61

goodbyes are never easy

but as hard as it is

bye for good.

messages
i should send

in my darkest moments, you shed light on my situation. you show me that growing isn't always pretty and that getting dirty is a part of the process. i like to think of myself as a seed that will one day bloom into a flower, but before that, i have to weather the conditions and make it out of the soil.

through the seasons of life, i'm tested. though i've lost petals, my roots remain strong. thorns have grown to protect me from trauma, yet somehow weeds still disguise themselves as friends. if i'm not careful, they will choke the life out of me. you gave me the discernment to recognize the ugly truth of poison ivy, but for some reason, i still see the beauty in her.

did you bring me here to leave me
to make an example out of me
to show people this is what happens
when you go for things out of reach
you'll have to turn around and start over

why me?
why this lesson?
did i ask for too much?
was i supposed to not dream so boldly?

incomparably, our conversations have been intimately watering. you listen attentively for hours as i let the ugly voice in my head pour out. although i know these things aren't true, i will continue to share them with you. you always remind me that a thought is just a thought. nothing more, unless i give it the power it thirstily craves. at that point, it will become a weed. ugly, tangled, desperate to become rooted, needing to be plucked. you emphasize that i have to give it that power because on its own, it has none. it's so insignificant that until i offer a seed of attention, it *doesn't even exist*.

you've been here
before every triumph, every success, every moment of joy
you've stood by me through every struggle, every journey,
every stretch of growth
you stayed after every heartbreak, every failure, every
mistake

you never left
you never will

you are the only constant in my life
and always have been

thank you for forgiving me
thank you for loving me
thank you for seeing me

i could never thank you enough
but still, thank you

there's nothing i could do that you wouldn't forgive
no matter how harsh i've acted, or how wrongly i've lived
even in my worst moments, you hold out your hand
you say the past has passed, it was a part of a plan
you provide a space of truth that lies can never go
you see the empty parts of me, and make them whole
you give me chance after chance,
even when i didn't deserve it
you remind me i still have so much life to live
i still have a greater purpose

71

how is it that you know every detail about me and still
love me
you love my ugly
you love my flaws
you love my imperfections
you love my all

parents are said to be our most powerful imprint
molding their children into the shape they will become
the coping styles
the patterns
all etched by their touch
this weight is so immense
this is the greatest responsibility a person will possess
what greater influence exists
than to create life
nurture it
watch it grow
and then
release it

you've been the greatest gift in my life
though ironically you gave it to me
you've never been perfect, but you were what i aspire to be
i aspire to be a reflection of you
and i hope that one day you'll be proud of me too
not for being like you but for just being who i am
every time i said *"i can't,"* you tell me *"you can"*
you were so unselfish, always putting me first
you saw the good in me, even at my worst
even in disappointment, you showed me grace
though you are a full person you always make space
you taught me the meaning of unconditional love
not the kind with stipulations, but the kind from above
you've always encouraged me when i was uncertain
you never ask for anything, just that i be my own person
you made me believe i could achieve my deepest desires
you've given me an example that i could never acquire
you're a living standard that is set so high
you gave me the very wings that allow me to fly
you are magnificent, incomparable,
overflowing with beauty
you have been the greatest by choice, not duty
~ *you are the best in the world*

there's nothing i could do to make you less proud
yet somehow i think differently
i've made a lot of mistakes
even if there were good intentions
though i've never been scared of you
i was always trying to hide
i didn't want you to see all the hurt
that i had buried inside
i only wanted you to see a perfect version of me
you never asked for perfection
and still, through every disguise
you see

me

i never understood how the two of you fell in love
you are complete opposites in every way
light and dark
water and fire
good and evil
the keeper of my dreams and ruler of my nightmares
i never witnessed the love between you
maybe by the time i was born it was too late
the sweet nothings had already turned
to bitter hate

you were supposed to be my first real love
but you never wanted me
was i a mistake
you sought to disown me
yet i inherited your whole face
was it fate?
was i your punishment?
your lesson in human form
i used to think you hated me
but maybe you hated the reflection
you hated me because i remind you of you
and it's hard to face yourself
trust me
i know

you never signed my birthday cards. why? is it because you had nothing to say?

for some reason, i always thought this was so odd. when i give birthday cards, i usually bleed out into them with ink, so to receive a card that said nothing,

said everything.

you were so empty, so numb, that you had no positive words for me. not once have you said you love me, or that i make you proud. most times, when you spoke to me, your mouth was full of disdain or disgust. often, it didn't even feel like the words you were saying were meant for me.

they were meant for you.

in spite of all the hateful things you said and did, i still wanted to make you proud, at least in the past.

i wanted you to validate me.

i wanted you to see me.

i needed to prove to you that your words had no power over me. and right now, i can say with certainty, they don't. and they never will...

again.

there aren't many things i carry regret for, but i was angry with you for a very long time. sometimes, i forgot you existed entirely, until your name came up in conversation. i tried to erase you from my memory. all the memories i do have are too painful to touch.

i needed you. even though you were physically there, you were *never really* there.

i carried quiet jealousy for those who had what i longed for. the kind of relationship i desperately craved. the one you never gave.

what had i done to deserve this? to inherit this torture? why me? why you? it doesn't even matter anymore. i never asked you. now, you are no longer here. it shocked me, the way i grieved you when you died. maybe i wasn't grieving you, but the version of you i wished for. the version i never got to know.

i'm not perfect
though i used to pretend to be
i used to put on versions of myself
just to people please
time and time again
i'd show up as someone else
then wonder why no one could see
how much i needed help

i searched my psyche for years, looking for an answer to what was weighing me down. why was i stuck repeating the same patterns and moments in different situations? carrying baggage full of shame, unable to offload completely. once i let one thing go, i picked up something else. as the years went by, i realized i was buying back the items i donated to the thrift store. things i willingly gave away, i searched for and brought back into my life as if they'd serve a different purpose.

it's like i was caught in a cycle i had created. i was stuck between the desire to heal and the comfort of familiar pain. every time i moved forward, fear and doubt whispered in my ear. they wished to weigh me down to the same spot. i've discovered it's not only hard to let go, but also hard to understand why you held on so tightly to begin with.

i can never apologize enough for what i did to you. if i could start over, i would do things differently. i hope one day you'll allow me to tell you that you deserved so much better from me. i'm sorry for not giving us a chance to grow. i can only imagine the memories we could have made and the love we could have shared. at the time, i thought i was making the best decision, the right decision. now i see it was only best for me. i didn't think about you. i didn't consider you. i was selfish. i chose everything over you, my career, my dreams, my future. i could see one where we would be together, but not right now. i saw a version of life where you were a part of it, but i didn't choose that life when it mattered. the joy you would have given me. i can only imagine. i've learned that some choices can't be undone, and some decisions can't be made right. no matter how well-intended, some decisions aren't the right choices at all.

i'm sorry you had no say, and i'm sorry i didn't realize it until it was too late.

withholding information is the same as lying
not telling the whole truth is just as conniving
trying to save my own skin, i kept hiding
i'm sorry for not showing the real me
i'm sorry for denying
i'm sorry for building walls instead of bridges
i'm sorry for being selfish in my decisions

they say *blood makes you family*
but that's not always true
because if that were enough we would've felt closer sooner
and yet some days i used to look at you
and think, *"how we could possibly be related"*
we were nothing alike
we didn't process the same
didn't dream the same dreams
didn't even hurt in the same ways
we shared a house, birthday cakes, matching outfits
and trauma that neither of us asked for
we silently grew side by side, parallel and opposite
like two trees with roots tangled beneath the soil
but branches outstretched toward different skies
the older i get, the more i understand what it means to be
cut from the same cloth
we were
we are
but we are the perfect example of how the same pain can
shape people into entirely different forms
for so long i thought our differences created distance
now i see they're a map
a story of how the mind bends to survive
we didn't come out the same
but we did come out strong, resilient, bonded
but not just by blood, but by the unspoken understanding
of what we've been through and how it's not who we are
and somehow, despite everything, we found each other in
the debris
and that's what makes us family

there is so much weight centered on romantic love. on finding *the one*, your soulmate, your twin flame, your person. the one you will build a life with, grow old with, be buried beside. but what about the ones who held your heart before you found forever or even knew what it meant? what about our friends? what happens to them? the ones who answered the 2 a.m. calls, the ones who heard what you were saying, even in your silence. the ones who didn't judge your mess, even though they wanted to. the ones who stayed through your ugly phase when nothing was pretty about you, nothing easy, nothing convenient. the ones who saw you when you didn't want to be seen, who loved you not because they had to, but simply because they did. they don't get a ring. they don't get a ceremony. no one gives them a gift for showing up and saving you, but they do. over and over, they do. we don't talk enough about this kind of love, at least i don't. the kind that doesn't ask for vows, but is loyal anyway. the kind that doesn't come with conditions, but with time, patience, and so many years shared. you may not be a "significant other," but you... are so significant. in the middle of chasing forever with someone, i'll never forget you because you helped me get there. and this type of love means more than i can ever emphasize.

i honestly can't imagine my life without you
when the world feels too heavy
you're one of the first people i call
with you i've opened doors i've kept locked for years
i've said things i've never dared speak out loud to anyone
because with everyone else i say "i don't want to talk
about it."
even though inside i'm screaming *please ask me again*
and you always do
you say "well, you can."
like it's the simplest thing in the world
like i'm allowed to be comforted
without needing to earn it
i ask you "do you have space?"
and somehow no matter what storm you're weathering
you always make room for mine
you've never made me feel like a burden
you've never made me feel too much
you just love me
as i am
where i am
and i can't express to you how rare that is
how healing
this is not ordinary or casual
this is true friendship
the kind people spend lifetimes praying for
and i get to have it
with you
thank you for making me feel like i'm never alone

one of the things i love most about you is that i never had to look for you. you just appeared in stylish fashion, like something i didn't know i needed until you were there. it still amazes me that we grew up in the same place, breathing the same air, surrounded by the same water, and somehow never crossed paths for so long. but when we did... it felt effortless... organic. like something that had been waiting to happen. i'm so thankful it did. our friendship reminds me of pasta, the kind that gets better with time; the longer it sits, the more it bakes, the flavors deepen, and the richness settles in. it's warm, comforting, filled with little intricate details that only time could uncover.

you've always been the boldest spirit i know. there's a fire in you that i also have, and i admire that. *the kill,* i call it. you speak your mind. you live with your whole heart, like you're not afraid to expose it. and that kind of courage wakes something up in me. something i didn't even realize was asleep.

when i first started facing my shame, you were the only person i trusted with it. the first one i thought, *if she thinks i'm a bad person after this... then i truly am.* i wish i could say people's words don't affect me, and most of the time they don't. but yours... yours hold weight, because they come from a place i respect, from you.

and maybe i'll never be able to fully explain what that means, but i hope you feel it. i hope you know how much it means to be seen by you, and just know

i see you.

you are such a dreamer, and that's where our souls find each other. in the place between what is, what could be, what will be, we meet. our conversations about wanting more and being more nourishes something deep in me that others just don't reach. whenever i start feeling like i'm asking for too much, you appear like magic and say, *ask for more, go bigger, go bolder, why not?* you've never been one for boxes or masks. you've never let people tell you who to be. you look at the rules, the standards, the expectations, and tear them up in everyone's faces and write your own. if i'm being honest, i can't remember when we became friends. there wasn't a single moment. it just feels like you've always been here. like we were always meant to be woven into each other's lives. i champion you with everything in me. i want every desire you hold quietly to be yours loudly! not because you earned it (which you have) but because you deserve it simply by being who you are. what amazes me is how you dare to think beyond yourself. how you see the bigger picture and still act with love. your heart is a photograph of a better world. and the way you pour into our community, the way you speak life into the very ground that raised you... it makes me proud. i'm honored to know you. yet still, it makes me angry to know some people around you can't see it. they're blind to the beauty you carry. the light you bring, the rare jewel that you are. one day they'll look back and realize you were the thing they searched for all along. i just hope by then you've already given that light to someone and something that sees it clearly, the way i always have.

people say it's hard to make friends as an adult. i think it's hard to keep the original ones because, as children, things are easy. there are no egos, no trauma, no baggage. you haven't even figured out how trauma will change you. you're blessed if you happen to retain friends that see you in the many seasons of life. most won't stay. they'll have seen your best but also your worst. the mistakes you've made. maybe they'll call you out or simply remove themselves quietly and say, *"we just grew apart."* and maybe that's true. but it's hard to give up on something that meant so much.

this friendship is sacred. you've seen my origin story, and though you had the opportunity to leave, you stayed around through my highs and lows. i could talk to you endlessly, reliving the mountains of memories in our past, and we would never run out of peaks. i know we have gotten older, and a lot of things have changed. we're not kids anymore. but i'm excited to get to know you all over again. this time as adults.

89

you're the ivory to my ebony. perfect harmony, even in our contrast. when i think of us, i think of laughter. the kind that makes your face hurt. the kind that makes your eyes tear up. even writing this, i can't help but smile. because you've brought so much joy to my life. from dancing in your driveway, sweating off our "x's," car concerts, long walks with no destination.

you've always been down for the ride, no matter where it led.

time has moved so fast, but you were there for the beginning of so much.

you never laughed at my dreams. never made me feel strange for wanting things no one could see but me. that means everything. people are quick to label us as too much or too odd, but you are a place where i can fully be myself. you feel like family to me. you are family to me, and no matter how long it's been, we always pick up like no time has passed. there's something about you, you're warm. you're welcome. you feel like home. you're sensitive, just like me. you feel deeply, and that's not a weakness it's strength.

i love how you say *"i'm trying my best."* just know you've always been your best to me.

it's a rare thing to have friends for the majority of your life, because sometimes, even after all the years shared, you realize how much you still don't know about each other. we are constantly learning. it's like we started off with an empty dictionary, and together we filled in the definitions, but as life changed, the meanings changed.

through the years, we have evolved in immense ways. sometimes, we didn't even acknowledge it out loud for some time. i didn't know how to communicate these things, and i feel even in silence, we understood each other.

there are moments in my life i wish i had the opportunity to rewrite, and a very hard one is tied to you. i've made choices i'm not proud of. even when i tried to *"act mature"* and do everything right, i still ended up hurting you.

that's something i have carried with me. it's one thing to be hurt, and another to realize i was the one that caused it. and for that, i've felt guilt and shame.

i've always tried to hold myself to a higher standard. to be someone people can count on, but with you, i fell short.

even when i came to you, you showed me grace. even if you didn't mean it, and even though i didn't deserve it, you did.

i appreciate your forgiveness, and now i have to forgive myself.

there aren't words big enough
to describe this feeling
you breathe fresh air into me
that is so healing
you are a good listener
warm and kind
you speak honestly
always say what's on your mind
even though sometimes it's not what i want to hear
you try to be direct
and make things clear

you have an immaculate vision for your life
that's another thing about you i really like
you are ambitious and witty
generous and giving
you are open and full of room to receive
you provide a comfort i so deliberately need
you have so many layers that i'd love to peel
the deeper i go, the more that appeals

you are real

all your secrets i want to conceal
but know with me, you can reveal

i am here
ready to love you

i miss you.
i can't think of anything else
when i'm with friends or alone
i long for your presence
my ears burn for your voice
my eyes seek to behold you.
with you, i feel safe
not alone or out of place
i feel at home.

you gave me a feeling words can't explain
a desire so big my heart can't contain
a fever so hot it can't be tamed
you ignite in me a love flame

you are my muse
when i need inspiration
you are the source i use
every attribute of you

is special

so sometimes it's hard to choose
should i focus on your eyes
and their beautiful hues
i could concentrate on your lips
and the way they speak what's true
or what about your hands
and the way they leave me touched
or maybe your electric smile
and cute little blush
you are never too much
you are always enough
you are my muse

is love truly blind?
am i the person you dream of when you close your eyes?
the first thought that comes to your mind?
do you see me for who i truly am?
not my skin, hair, body
i hope you can embrace me
and my flaws
heal my sorrows
and accept me
sins and all
i am not perfect
but in your eyes you see i'm worth it
worthy with purpose
my value isn't determined
by my surface
or service

i lied.

i know i said it's fine
now i'm sitting ruminating
your words on repeat replaying
can't get you off my mind
have i just been wasting all my time
wishing
you
were mine

talking for hours, sharing intimacies and intricacies of our
lives just to not know each other

again

will i ever be enough for you?

no.

what you're looking for isn't in me, and frankly has
nothing to do with me. you are seeking validation that i
cannot give a sign, an affirmation, a reason to live. you
need to look inside yourself, because you have the answer
you need. stop hurting people, and stop using me to feed
your ego. to make you feel wanted.

yes, i want you

but it's not fair
you are unresponsive
you are never there
and you are emotionally unavailable
to my calls

i can't trust you with my body
i won't let you take control
i don't trust you with my spirit
i don't trust you with my soul
you treat me like an object
like something you can own
you think i have a price tag
and that i can be sold

i am more than surface
more than curves and skin
my story runs deep
hidden quietly within

when you ask what my lips do...
wouldn't you love to know
but i don't kiss snakes who bite
then slither off when life gets cold

your lies are unraveling
i see scales through your smile
i see the games you play
i have for a while

you can no longer wrap yourself around me
or trick me with your schemes
you say one thing...
but i know exactly what you mean

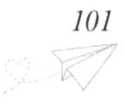

choosing me seems simple and uncomplicated
sadly i am mistaken
you see i'm distracted by handsome faces
strong arms pretty teeth
mouths full of empty promises and deceit
kisses drenched in lies and eyes
that never actually meet mine
because in fact

you
don't
see
me

you look at me with lust
at my breast my hips and butt
but never once
did you look to see who i truly am
and do you care? does it matter?
date after date you flatter
feed me
breadcrumb me
with the expectation
you are paying for more than just a meal
in some way my body is an expected part of the deal
but i am not for sale

i could literally throw up my heart
"*should have listened to my intuition from the start*"
i was wandering, lost in the dark
there's something about you... i just felt a spark

in no space
in no universe
in no time
were we *ever* meant to only be friends

your eyes are the most beautiful oceans of love
i've ever swum in
and sometimes i forget to come up for air
lost in the depths of your soul far from meaningless care
where silence speaks louder than words ever could
i sink deep into your psyche where i am understood

how can i heal your heart
when mine is in remission?
i don't want to speak empty promises
or lie to you in kisses
i'm trying to heal
but for some reason i don't want to let you go
while i stitch myself back together

your heartbeat plays the most beautiful love ballad
but i can no longer string you along
i'm sorry for dragging this out
for playing all the chords
starting a new song
when i had no intention to finish writing it with you

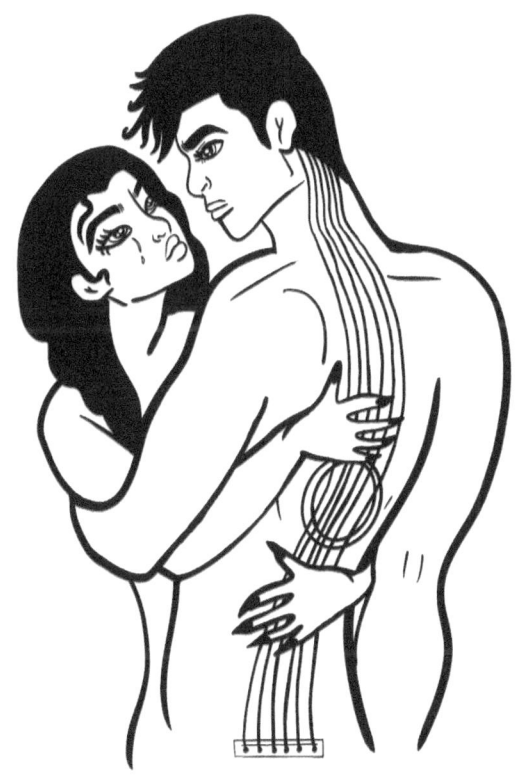

your pulse feels like a song
one i've danced to over and over
i've played continuously
i know the rhythm by heart
the beat of its drum slowing and quickening
always pulling me back in
as i pull away

i can't keep changing myself for you
so it's over yes we're through
this might feel sudden like it came out the blue
but i left this relationship in my mind
long before my body withdrew

i'm not one to lie
i don't play pretend
i won't show up wearing a mask
with a forced smile ever again
i know it hurts but this isn't new
i've felt this way for a while and you have too

you saw this coming so don't act banal
always picking fights so deep in denial
i'm not here to judge this isn't a trial
but those tears you shed
are tears of crocodile

109

you feel different
i believe in second chances
i think we are allowed to change our minds
and often we are simply scared
that something can actually be
good for us
i understand your hesitation
how can you trust someone that says all the right things?
doing precisely what you want in exact ways
can you trust me?
i hope so
because you deserve to be treated well
and i want to be the one who does

we fit together

you were the missing piece to my puzzle i didn't know
needed solving

it's interesting
life is ever changing how we move though seasons and
phases we try to make things work
people, beliefs, dreams, careers
and some things do for a time
but in other instances things start to feel out of place
and before you know it we are no longer aligned

but

you're not like that
you are flexible
you evolve
you are excited by change
i use to think things that were permanent were literally
unmovable but everything that is solid is flexible in its
permanence that's what makes it enduring
that's what you are

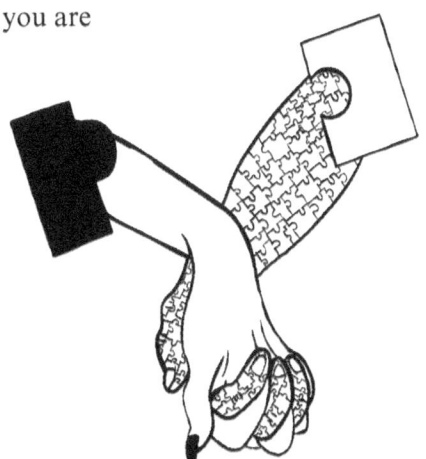

tiffany gregory

i thought i had more time
i kept thinking "tomorrow i'll reach out... tomorrow"
i dragged my feet. i kept waiting for the right moment to
fix what was broken between us
but time doesn't wait
it didn't

now it's gone
now your gone

i use to think time was infinite
that there was always more time

more chances to say *i love you*

more moments to say *i'm sorry*

i forgive you

i'm proud of you

you mattered to me

but life doesn't work like that

i thought i had more time
but now i have none

at least not with you

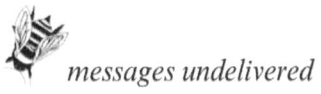

i've been wanting to talk to you about all the things we never did. all the words left unsaid buzzing around in my head.

but what use would it do?

in the end, talking to you felt like talking to a stranger. you weren't the person i'd been with all this time. when i looked into your eyes, i saw nothing, no warmth, no compassion. what happened to all the feelings that were once there? the feelings that we shared? somehow, they slipped away like pollen blown off petals. but when? you didn't give me a warning at all. you just took from me what you once willingly gave. you left me feeling confused, used, unwanted, and this isn't the first time. so this stung differently than before. somehow, the sweet honey of your voice turned to venom on your lips. i was left aching, not from the sting but from the memory of how gently you use to land on me.

i can feel you draining my energy
sucking the light out of me
to replenish your own
but what about me
will you ever pour into me
the way you take so freely
i won't allow myself to become dim
so you can shine brighter
especially when there's enough room
for the both of us the glow

i'm not quite sure what it is about you. maybe it's the way you came out of nowhere, unexpected and impossible to ignore.

it's the mystery of you, that draws me in. along the way, i started to think you only wanted one thing. you dragged on as if you cared. like you needed to keep pretending. maybe because you needed to save face.

you confuse me more than i can say. i still can't decide if you were playing me on purpose the entire time, or you caught feelings accidentally and ran scared. honestly, those seem like the only choices.

i refuse to believe you liked me, then lost feelings. i don't believe connection fades away like that. to me, connection isn't something you lose but abandon, and there's a difference. to lose something means you misplaced it with hopes to find it again, but to abandon something is to willingly walk away.

you chose not to make an effort or be consistent while i was reaching for you. yeah, you carried conversation, but only to reply and not to connect.

why couldn't you simply let me in? why didn't you feel safe with me? i'm the one who listened, who asked the hard questions, who tried to bring out the parts of you that you hid away, and still you walked away.

if you have to disappear to feel seen...
leave

when i realized i was more afraid of losing you
than afraid of losing me
i knew i had to let you go
and set myself free

messages
to me

i pray one day you'll learn to be motivated by the things
you love versus the ones that hurt you.

rejection isn't always about you
what an odd picture and point of view
it's hard not to inspect your reflection
and search for what may be disconnected
it has to be me? what did i do?
why am i not good enough for you?
these thoughts tend to cloud my head
and overshadow what was *actually said*
you explained what's on the page
and in between the lines i read
dissociation takes over... ughh, not again
stay present, allow yourself to feel
is this happening? what's actually real?
i was listening, but other things were heard
stay on this page, no need to turn...*this hurts*
how can i not take this personally?
i'm just a person, and this is addressed only to me
i'm tired of the ache
 i'm tired of trying
when i put myself out there i end up left crying
my eyes swell and my heart quakes
was giving love a try another mistake?
because i'm shook
and quite frankly,
maybe i should consider shelving this book.
it's become painfully hard to write
it's hard to keep giving pieces of me
glamorizing what could be
only to be woken up from a sweet dream
and thrown into this reality
that it may have all been in my imagination

i didn't even notice when depression snuck in
wrapped itself around my neck and settled within
sadness filled me deep and uncontrollably
dragging me down quiet and slowly
waking up in silence no one else around
spending entire days without a single sound
when i finally saw someone, it wasn't connection
it was more of a transaction lacking affection
i really just wanted someone to care
to be present and sit with me there
and not for what i have to give
some days it feels like no one cares if i die or i live
as if i am insignificant and invisible
my worth attached to a fictional visual
instead of what's inside
images of perfection they've chosen to find
and i'm left here completely dismissed
wondering, did i ever really exist?

it's ok to be sad
but don't unpack and stay
it's ok to be down
but don't end that way
you are so strong
you are so tough
you were made to win
you are enough

being alone will always be better than being with someone who doesn't have room for you.

loneliness is often just a matter of perception. it's actually a blessing. you have the freedom to live life entirely on your terms, without needing someone's permission. you get to build a universe that is entirely yours, full of galaxies and constellations born from imagination and creativity.

and when someone special does come along, maybe you'll choose to share your world with them. but even then, remember you are already vast because you created something beautiful and whole all on your own.

feeling lonely is a strange occurrence
like the tides i'm being pushed and pulled with the
current...
events that is
mind empty
heart aching
blood boiling
mouth shaking
on the verge of a panic attack
take a deep breath
just relax
close your eyes
and picture a calm ocean under a sunny sky
relax
remember what's true
you are exactly where you are supposed to be
relax
yes to be
living in the moment presently
because once it's gone you'll never have it again
a chance to relive a chance to begin
relax
you are all you need
inside you is loneliness's remedy
your self-esteem the power within
you are your greatest love interest and friend
trust yourself to show up
time and time again
~ *lonely mess*

failure tried to visit and shadow me in defeat
layered with lies wrapped in deceit
grief followed death like a lingering ghost
love came and left when i needed it most

sweet words given but only at a price
lullaby lies serenaded so nice
old chapters closed without warning or grace
new pages left blank, but how do i fill the empty space?

i'm at a point where i don't want to feel
because feeling everything makes nothing feel real
there were some good moments right after a trial
but the pain hurts so much i could barely smile
i survived the storm but forgot to be grateful
been waiting so long i lost how to be faithful
anger sits where peace used to dwell
an unfamiliar fire that i know too well

now i'm handling my soul like delicate tea
learning the strength in patience and clarity
sip too fast and you might get burned
but wait, be patient, and the taste of love will return

you have the biggest heart be careful with who you share it
not everyone has honest intentions
some will take your warmth and leave you cold
suck the youth from you and drain your soul
leave you feeling like you don't matter
and it's hard to see until after
so guard your heart under lock and key
and give it to the ones that gently set it free

i knew something had to change when i started getting my heart broken by people i never loved.

maybe it's not about them. maybe this is about me. why am i so willing to give so much of myself so soon? making all this space and reserving all this room hoping, someone will stay.

sometimes the emptiness people leave feels heavier than the weight their presence ever did.

i can't keep making the same mistakes. confusing attention with affection.

so before anyone else even has the choice or chance to leave, i'll choose me.

choosing yourself comes with a lot of goodbyes
not just to people but to versions of you that thought
just enough was enough

don't be afraid to say what's in your heart
even if you think it's not what others want to hear
people who want to understand
are the only ones with open ears

my wealth is more than material
it's not counted in dollars and things
it's measured in peace
in love that asks for nothing in return
in moments that money could never buy

i'm rich in laughter shared
in safe silence
in memories that warm my soul

what i carry is not for sale and cannot be spent
it's paid in patience not in gold
in joy
in knowing that i already have enough
in knowing that i already am enough

you are art
you are a beautiful creation
crafted by the original maker
you are lava poured into love
cascading over this flesh
to form mountains of joy
rivers of emotions
curls filled with curiosity
and filled with an energy so vibrant
the sun squints

is there anything that's truly original? a thought, an idea, a creation... or does everything come from something? have i had one unique thought?

yes.

sure, everything comes from something but even if different pieces come from the world around you, the way you build it is uniquely yours. two people can draw from the same inspiration and create completely different art. what's the difference?

you.

you are unique. you are a creator. even if you are inspired, what you produce has never existed quite like this. so, trust that your voice, your vision, your gifts matter. be confident your art has meaning and deserves to be shared.

surround yourself with souls
who burn as brightly as you
who love deeply
dream boldly
and show up with the same fire in their hearts
that lives in yours

you know you can do better
yet you are waiting for a sign
listen to your intuition
it's a mindful guide

you know you should leave
when the thought of it makes you feel relieved
who knows better than you
what you actually need

once you heal you'll stop
mistaking crumbs for a feast
you'll stop accepting
excuses dressed as apologies
empty words wrapped in charm
lust disguised as love
beautiful lies whispered like lullabies
and promises that only live in some
distant imagined future
healing teaches you what your heart is truly worth
and that *"almost love"*
is never enough

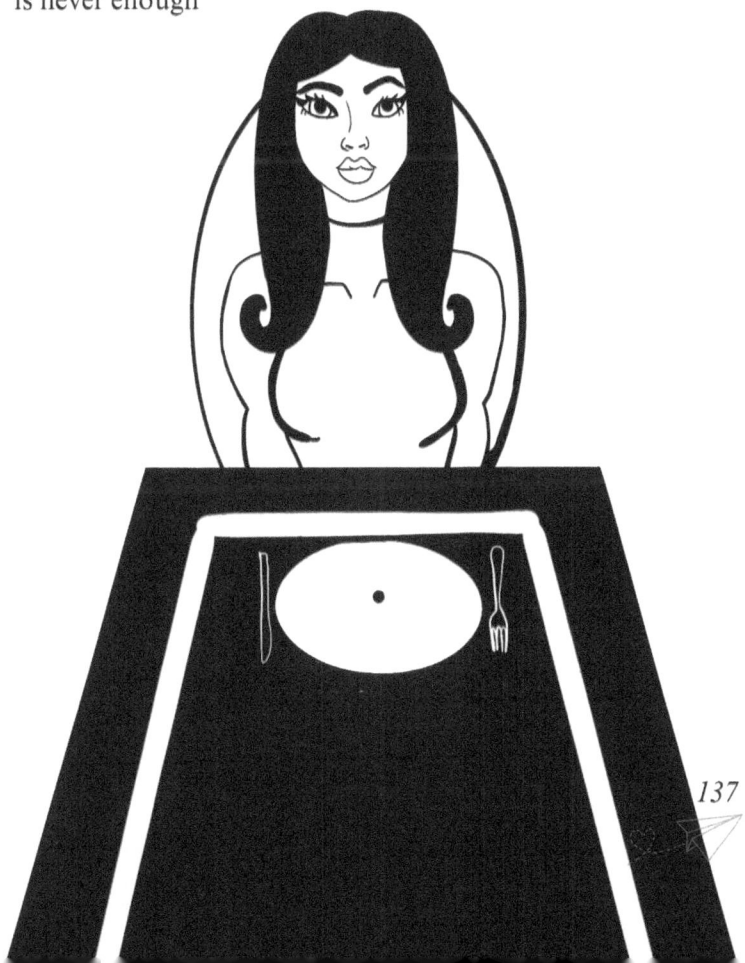

regardless of how broken you feel
you aren't
you are strong
pick up the pieces and repair
you have been here before
trauma disguised as romance affects you so interestingly
it seems it leaves bruises you try to cover with smiles
why be afraid to display your wounds?
is it because they still hurt or because they are still open?

you are a dream addict
a believer
a soul ignited in lust for life
intoxicated by the rush of becoming
inspiration fills your veins
giving you a high no substance could ever match
self-expression is your air
art is your language
they take you to places people fantasize
don't believe the people who tell you
your dreams are too big
they aren't bigger that you
think of them as clothing
not too large just not yet fitted
you'll grow into them
you have so much to give
so much life to live
and the power you have within
is bursting at the seams
waiting to be released

you are magnetic
things are attracted to you
good and bad
light and shadows
blessings and lessons

your discernment is a compass
let it guide your decisions

not everything and everyone is meant for you to keep
some things are meant to reveal themselves and then be
thrown to the abyss
while others are meant as companions to journey with you
along the way

regardless every mess is a message

i often overthink

i can't help but plan out everything
my mind plays out all possibilities like chess
mapping my next three moves and theirs
the possibilities and directions are endless
but people sometimes trap themselves
in that little square
in an old pattern
in the black and white
and that makes them easy to read

i no longer want people who don't want me. i don't want to play games. i've noticed they say similar things about me. they say i have a pull, something that draws them in. maybe it's my positivity or light, and when they are bathed in this energy, they are in bliss.

i make them feel wanted, comfortable, seen, and heard. but the moment i step into the light, a switch happens for them, and suddenly, i am a human with needs, who feels insecurities. the fantasy fades, and for the first time they see me clearly, and they leave.

no one that is truly for me will see me and leave.

ever.

everyone is not going to like you
if they do
it's because you aren't being honest
the truth doesn't aim to please
the truth aims to free

you are exactly where you are supposed to be. often, you feel you are behind. but behind who?

your peers
your timeline
your expectations
it feels like you've come so far just to be pulled backwards.

like you ran full speed in the wrong direction. you start to question, *have i failed every single test thrown, but wrapped it in false perception ?*

no.

that's not the truth. that's the voice of doubt. the kind that disguises itself as logic. feeding on fear and shame. this voice is a liar. catch it when it comes and replace it with what's true.

you are not lost
you are not late
you are progressing
you are becoming

when i first moved to los angeles, i would run every morning and then walk back home. on those walks, i would say the things i was grateful for out loud, no matter how small. i took in everything around me. i wanted to remember every moment. my phone quickly filled with pictures of beautiful flowers, swaying palm trees, and endless skies painted with colors that transformed every day. those simple moments gave my day purpose and life. i was full of joy. one of my deepest dreams had finally come true. i would say to myself, "look at where you are. look how far you've come!"

but over time, i stopped voicing my gratitude. i stopped taking photos of flowers and skies. my feet hit the pavement with racing thoughts; my eyes only checked the clock as i ran my miles that felt heavy and empty. the journey i once woke up for and looked forward to, had become just *another thing*. some *thing* to check off my long list for the day. it was a burden. so much so, at one point i stopped running altogether.

it took time, but i had to open my eyes to the doubt that had quietly blinded me. i forgot that my race isn't a sprint. life takes time, and along the way, there is so much beauty waiting to be noticed. i want that again. sure, i know everything isn't pretty, and hard times offer perspective. those moments also offer lessons, but choosing to hold on to the good just feels like a better path, a better way. i've realized no matter how broken or tired i feel, i can't lose hope. i can't lose gratitude. i can't stop seeing the beauty in life. i can't stop.

you can have it all
maybe not all at once but you can have them
your dreams, a career, love, happiness, peace, everything
you can have anything
because you are everything

my birthday is like my own personal new year, but in the last few years, just days before the date arrives, sadness takes the driver's seat and steers me straight into what i like to call "a moment."

a moment of reflection... and lies.

another year slipped away, another mark added to the timeline of my life, another year of goals unfinished, dreams that didn't come true, another year of missed opportunities, another year spent feeling alone.

why do i do this to myself? why do i ruminate and sit in the emptiness of what's missing instead of standing in the fullness of what's here? i am alive. i am still here. that alone is one of the greatest gifts from God. what a blessing it truly is to grow older, to wake up and gain wisdom and knowledge, to learn, to love, to keep trying, to still have something i aspire to, work towards.

it's ok to be driven, but where? sometimes i get so focused on the destination that i forget to celebrate the journey. the truth is, there were many things i did this year that i never did stop to acknowledge, never paused to be proud of.

and maybe that's what i need to do now: to remember i have been growing. even when it didn't feel like it was enough, it was something, and that something matters. this year i choose to meet my birthday with grace and deep gratitude. i'm not behind. i am becoming, and that's worth celebrating!

147

speak life into your life
shine light over the night
spread love where there is pain
share peace without gain
let your presence soften the room
your words become what blooms
stand firm, but be kind
lead with heart, not just with mind

you've made mistakes
you are not one
forgive yourself
let go of the lie that you are unworthy of it
don't let shame take root where growth is meant to
blossom

is this moment eternal
is this moment permanent
is this moment lasting
don't make a definitive choice
off your temporary feelings
let emotion rise
but don't let them decide
clarity will come
when the chaos subsides

not everything you do has to be shared
some things are just for you
quiet victories
sacred moments
silent healing

you don't have to post every win
explain each boundary
prove something to others

your joy doesn't need an audience to be real
not everything needs to be witnessed to be confessed
some of the most meaningful moments are the ones only
you will ever know

don't feel compelled to give everyone all of you
even if you were compressed they still couldn't hold you
your depth wasn't made for shallow hands
your light wasn't created to be dimmed
you are not fragments to be passed around
you are whole
you are not for everyone
and rejection is God's protection

you are complex, but easy to understand.

you bless everyone you meet
your presence brings peace
your words give ease
your touch heals need
your smile shines bright
your love sheds light
your breath gives life
to the world you feel right

you are anointed for greatness
everyone else sees it
open your eyes instead of closing them
when you look in the mirror
start seeing what's clearly visible

your seeds of inspiration will bloom
into flowers of realization
continue to water them
let your tears of hope
shine on them with the joy of endless possibilities
and nurture them with words of affirmation

to walk you have to crawl
to reach new heights sometimes you fall
there are days when we feel so small
but being big doesn't make you strong
we take on new form from the day we are born
from the moment of first breath
we change until death
from shedding old skin
cutting off dead ends
letting go of parts of ourselves so we can begin again
we all have those days
when things don't go our way
it's going to be alright yes you'll be okay
if you feel afraid of change don't be dismayed
after a stormy night the sky will give way
and a new you will bloom from a gloomy cocoon tomb
because sometimes to feel alive something inside has to die

don't let the harshness of the world harden your heart
remain gentle and pure
remain patient and steady
not all energy is made for you to take up
some you need to reject and not take in
because it will change your spirit to match its own

romantic relationships are starting to feel unfulfilling
but what are you looking for them to fill?
you need to be full all on your own

there's nothing wrong with desiring love but if it's at the expense of you it'll never be worth it

i'm excited for the person you are growing into
the strength you are building
the softness you are protecting
you see the mountaintop in the distance
but the path feels unclear
keep climbing
keep reaching
remember to celebrate the wins along the way
the small victories
sometimes you speed through the climb so fast
you don't even realize you're back on the ground
because you are on to the next peak
growth isn't just in reaching
it's in resting
reflecting
reconnecting
and remembering

remember
you are rich
you are abundant
you are overflowing
you are wealthy
not just in material things
but eternal things
love
wisdom
light
resilience

you are not forgotten
you are unforgettable

give yourself the grace
you so easily share with others
gentle words
second chances
patience

give yourself the space
you so freely give to them
to breathe
to break
to begin
to build
without guilt or shame

give yourself the love
you pour so tenderly into everyone
the kind that stays
the kind that grows
the kind that whispers *you are enough*

you deserve the same gentleness
you give so effortlessly
let it return home to you
let it live in you

dreaming is so exhilarating
limitless, free
but waking up is scary
because once your eyes are open
how do i make the dream real?
just know you can
the vision was planted in your mind for a reason
not randomly
it's not impossible
it's already done
it's already yours in another universe
waiting for you to catch up
just walk into it with confidence
not with fear
but with faith
one step at a time
one choice
one risk
one yes
then another
you don't have to know how
just believe

you are allowed to be
whatever and whoever you want to be
don't let the expectations of everyone else
tell you what type of you... you are supposed to be
just feel
just be free
to give
to express
all of you
you are not too much
you are not too loud
you are not too intense
you are whole and some people can't handle that

what would be the point of holding on to it anyway
in the end you can't take it with you so give it all you got
be bold enough to dream big and live bigger

just know it's ok to feel.
when you are sad you often
tell yourself "don't be sad"
but why not?
you wouldn't tell someone "don't be happy"
why silence the sorrow
and only recognize the joy

just feel
all of it
let it move through you
instead of building up inside

your feelings are real
your feelings are valid
they don't need permission
they need presence

there is beauty in the sunshine
there is beauty in the rain
even the sky has to cry sometimes

it's ok to feel them both
the light and the storm
laughter and pain

this is how you stay whole

you are greatness in human skin
that's not pride but truth that sits within
speak your dreams into the air
and watch them blossom everywhere

some days i'm just in awe of you
you don't look like what you've been through
you are so full of dreams, love, and beautiful things
your heart is like a garden
and the seeds of your soul will bloom into the
magnificence that's in your heart

i'm so proud of you
somehow through it all
you haven't let the hurt harden you
you remain kind
even when it's easier not to
you remain open
even when it's easier to turn away
you remain peaceful
even when the world is in chaos
you remain graceful
even when pain weighs heavy on your chest
you are a miracle
a dream refusing to fade
existing in reality
you are extraordinary
a gem whose brilliance illuminates

there's so much i need to tell you
now i'm pressing send
you have no idea how loved you are
you are your greatest friend

there's so much i need to tell you
now i'm pressing send
your dreams aren't too big
keep believing in them

there's so much i need to tell you
now i'm pressing send
you are not your mistakes
show yourself grace and know you're forgiven

there's so much i need to tell you
now i'm pressing send
you don't need external validation
everything you have been searching for
is within

about the author

Tiffany Gregory is a creator, writer, director, producer, recording artist, host, and actress who brings words to life both visually and verbally. Each of these roles shaped the depth and emotional range she now brings to her work as an author. In her debut collection, *Messages Undelivered*, she pairs poetry with illustrations to create an intimate and immersive reading experience.

This collection marks the beginning of Tiffany's journey as a *self-published* poet and author. It explores themes of love, loss, healing, and the weight of unspoken words. These are the letters never sent, buried confessions uncovered, and quiet truths she whispered to herself. Inspired by her personal experiences navigating heartbreak, trauma, grief, love, and renewal, each chapter delivers raw, honest, and deeply human messages.

Tiffany believes that poetry is the language of the heart, an art form that reveals our truest selves. Originally from Portsmouth, Virginia, she is now based in Los Angeles, California, where she continues to create, write, and inspire through her art.